7 Principles to Love Again

7 Principles to Love Again

Overcome the Pain, Learn the Lesson, and Love Again

Marcel D. Fears

XULON PRESS

Xulon Press
2301 Lucien Way #415
Maitland, FL 32751
407.339.4217
www.xulonpress.com

Paperback ISBN-13: 978-1-6628-0965-1
Hardcover ISBN-13: 978-1-6628-1232-3
Ebook ISBN-13: 978-1-6322-1684-7

Thank you

To my Lord and Savior Jesus Christ who counted me faithful putting me into the ministry. To my amazing family, and a special thank you to the greatest church in the world that I'm favored to Pastor, Overcomer's Life Church.

Dedication

This book is dedicated to my amazing, brilliant, and loving wife, whose real-life example of love, patience, and forgiveness was my inspiration for this work.

Thank you, Venus L. Fears.

What Leaders Are Saying

Pastor Joseph V. Parker Jr - Senior Pastor of Faith Fellowship Church, Memphis, TN / Influencer

Pastor Marcel Fears has written a must-read for anyone that desires to experience love God's way. Read this book to love again the right way!

Dr. Mary L Webster Moore - Educator / Author / CEO of A Moore Excellent Way Personal and Professional Development Institute

In a time of such marital turmoil and the personal pain that results from it, resources such as 7 Principles to Love Again are much needed. Pastor Marcel has been gifted with revelatory insights and a unique ability to connect them to people's lives in practical ways. It is my hope that this latest project will bless your life or that of someone you know and love, who needs the restoration it offers.

Pastor Micaiah Young - Author / Senior Pastor of The Life Center Church, Milwaukee, WI

Pastor Marcel Fears is an anointed vessel whose voice speaks clearly a word of hope healing and restoration. He transparently shares nuggets from his personal journey while introducing biblical principles that individuals can apply to their lives for victorious living. My life has been blessed by Pastor Fears' ministry and I am confident that every person who reads 7 Principles to Love Again and listens to his teaching and preaching will be greatly impacted and changed for the better.

Pastor Anthony Thomas, Author / Educator / Senior Pastor of Calvary Covenant Church of Chicago / CEO of Thomas Consulting & Counseling Service, Inc.

7 Principles to Love Again is an applaudable work by Pastor Marcel Fears! Readers will appreciate the restorative approach and nature of this book to the extent that change should be an automatic response. Pastor Marcel has enclothed the reality of pain and heartbreak one experiences in life with his own personal, relevant experiences that make the 7 Principles to Love Again immediately applicable. Pastor Marcel is a fun author to work with, and this piece is a must read! A necessary tool for pastors and counselors.

Takeitha Carter - Author / CEO of Working The Dash, Inc. Memphis, TN / Evangelist

Overcoming. Loving. Healing. Living. The principles in this remarkable book are replete with rich, inspiring, and priceless tools. This book invites you into a warm space of valuable information, with outstanding resources to propel your journey of healing and loving again. From this guide, you will be destined to improve your overall quality of life as you activate these easy-to-understand pledges. Read and share this wonderful book. You will not be disappointed!

TABLE OF CONTENTS

Introduction

Throughout a lifetime, one will experience many hurts. Are all hurts created equal? Based on my experiences, no, they are not! Hurt has many faces, many names, and many places. Undoubtedly, we could all create a long list of culprits who have caused us pain, and more painful than hurt itself is the source of that hurt.

Sometimes we are offended by someone in the grocery store or the mall. People at work say things that vex us. Even a neighbor may cause frustration. Most of us recover rather quickly from such, but unfortunately, recovery is not the same when the pain is caused by those closest to our hearts, those we have come to love. Father issues hurt, mother wounds are painful, and relationship wounds can render us breathless.

No hurt rivals the pain caused by those we have loved at the level of the heart. Heart-level wounds create setbacks that are paralyzing and seem irreversible! Unfortunately, there are those who have had episode upon episode of such pain to the point that they have become numb to loving from their hearts. Their hearts become so guarded or blocked that loving again seems unfathomable. Who would want to sacrifice themselves to this degree?

The Message Bible renders Proverbs 4:23 like this, "Keep vigilant watch over our heart; that's where life starts." The heart is where the issues we face in our everyday lives have had a profound impact on how we feel, think, and react. Things happen around us every day, and, in many cases, we can fall victim to the negative results these encounters often yield.

The assaults experienced by an unguarded heart act as a poison to erode and destroy our ability to love purely and freely. Negative relationship encounters result in a closed heart that is not willing to love because of the pains they have produced. These encounters damage the heart so terribly that it needs healing to trust and to believe in true love again. Are you carrying the pain of past hurts? Are you still recovering from a compromised trust that has left you to nurse your wounds alone? Ultimately, the actual impact of the damages our hearts have undergone cannot be determined physically but instead by our inability to hope, to trust, to love, and to be loved. As painful as this may be, there is a lesson to be learned and healing to be received. I declare to you, overcome the pain and gain from experience. True love (the love of God) is the balm that will heal our hearts and cause us to love again.

7 Principles to Love Again is all about restoring or bringing proper clarity back to your ability to love. Within the next few pages, I will share seven God-inspired principles you can apply to those places in your heart that need healing. They are given in no particular order and certainly not exhaustive, yet through the study of God's Word and personal experience, I firmly believe these principles can be the catalyst to heartfelt change. My friends, it is time for you to enjoy a fresh start. God wants to teach you how to *Love Again!*

PRINCIPLE 1:

Do Not Chase
the Counterfeit

SOME OF US HAVE HAD A DISTORTED PICTURE of what real love is. When this occurs, we will sometimes pursue what we think love should be. Perhaps there was a particular way we experienced loved at one point in our lives that changed our perception of it. Maybe it was a form of abuse at the hands of someone who claimed to have loved us but had an ulterior motive in mind. The distortions that accompany such brokenness may have caused us to chase after what we perceived true love to be. Nevertheless, I offer this truth—God is love! In restoring clarity to our love lives, we must begin with the proper Source of love, God.

> WHEN WE HAVE NOT EMBRACED GOD AS LOVE
> AND THE PICTURE THAT *HE* CREATES, THEN WE
> ARE SURE TO CHASE THE COUNTERFEIT!

When we have not embraced God as love and the picture that *He* creates, then we are sure to chase the counterfeit! Note John's declaration in 1 John 4:7-8 (KJV), "Beloved, let us love one another: for love is of God, and every one that loveth is born of God and knoweth God. He that loveth not knoweth not God; for God is love." God not only shows love, but *He is* also *love*! His essence, the fabric of His being, His very make-up is love! Therefore, the identity of the believer is expressed by how we love. The first step in bringing clarity back to your love life is to put God first. Only then can you begin to *Love Again*!

There are many promises that God has predestined for our lives. God's love births these promises for us. I need you to know that there is something pure and exceptional in your future that is reachable because of God's love for you. In many cases, before we experience the promise, we are presented with a counterfeit version of it. *Don't chase it!*

Let's examine a story in the Bible about the life of Abram and Sarai. God promised Abram that he would be the father of many nations and that his descendants would be blessed. This promise was for him and his wife. However, upon reading Genesis 16, you will find that Sarai, feeling she was past her childbearing years, suggested Abram marry her handmaiden, Hagar, and bear children with her.

The relationship between Abram and Hagar did indeed result in the birth of a son, Ishmael. However, this was not God's ideal plan. Ishmael was not the promise! In the years that followed, just as God said, Sarai gave birth to the promised son, Isaac.

Because of her eventual jealousy of Hagar, Sarai demanded that she and Ishmael leave the house. With a resentful heart, Hagar departed. Herein lies a great example of chasing the counterfeit. Abram and Sarai agreed for Abram to have a child with Hagar, creating an unhealthy and bitter relationship resulting in emotional wounds and loss of love for Hagar and Ishmael. When we learn to wait for God's promises for our lives and choose not to pursue counterfeits, we will avoid the pain and bitterness that illegitimate relationships may produce for us and others.

> WHEN WE LEARN TO WAIT FOR GOD'S PROMISES FOR OUR LIVES AND CHOOSE NOT TO PURSUE COUNTERFEITS, WE WILL AVOID THE PAIN AND BITTERNESS THAT ILLEGITIMATE RELATIONSHIPS MAY PRODUCE FOR US AND OTHERS.

When I Saw Her:

Taking a glance back over my life, I realized that for most my teen and young adult years, I spent a lot of time attempting to understand and settle into who I was as a person and young man. I'm sure many of you can relate to this process of "finding yourself," the process of self-discovery. That's why our support system and home life are so vitally important during this time because we are impacted, whether negatively or positively, by those around us. I literally spent years working to understand what I like and don't like, my tastes and my preferences, and even my personal style. It's a project of searching, a discovery opportunity, an intense scavenger hunt of learning yourself. When I began to mature in the understanding of myself, my standards, and my character, I also determined what behaviors, relationships, and interactions were acceptable and unacceptable for me. You see, when you are void of knowing who you are as a person, you can put yourself in the vulnerable and compromising position of accepting anything into your heart. Accepting "anything" is very dangerous. What may be good for one may not be good for another. We must

embrace and understand who we are as individuals. When

we embrace who we are, we won't compromise our convictions or negotiate our standards.

Finding a mate and a life-long love relationship with someone can look like an impossible task. It's scary for a lot of people. All kinds of questions and apprehensions may arise in our minds. Questions like, *Can I truly love this person with all my heart? Can I put my trust in another person who has the ability to turn and hurt me and totally damage my heart? Will our relationship last?* Or simply, *Is this the right one for me?*

I was in high school when I first laid eyes on her. I was figuring out who I was as most high school teenagers do. It took me years before I actually said one word to her. Just like a lot of church kids, we met in...yep, you guessed it, church. For a few years, it seemed as if we were going our separate ways and living our lives. Learning the world of dating, figuring out personalities, and failing miserably in love attempts, I needed every one of those moments to be able to recognize the right one for me when I saw her. Then one Saturday evening at...yep, church again, I saw her. Venus was her name, and this time, I was determined to speak up. She was just as beautiful as the first time I had seen her. After that day, I never let her go, and over seventeen years, two amazing sons, and an electric bill or two later, we're still here and still in love. As I pause and consider my relationship journey, I appreciate more and more the time I needed before Venus and I reconnected on that Saturday evening. I needed time to make mistakes and fail at other relationships.

I DESPERATELY NEEDED TO BE CRUSHED SO THAT
I COULD BE FASHIONED AND SHAPED IN THE
HANDS OF THE GREAT POTTER TO EXPERIENCE
THE REAL LOVE THAT MY HEART DESIRED.

I needed to experience the pain of heartbreak and feel the frustration of disappointment. I desperately needed to be crushed so that I could be fashioned and shaped in the hands of the great Potter to experience the real love that my heart desired. It's a fascinating thing that often, pain accompanies success because pain keeps us from taking the wrong road of destruction. The breaking of your spirit is what leaves the bitter taste of the counterfeit in your mouth so that you can recognize what's real. You have a story, as well, and like me, it doesn't feel good to feel lost or to experience hurt and disappointment. The power and truth of the matter is that God has a way of adjusting our vision and ordering our steps so that we can embrace what is true, beautiful, and authentic. Specific areas of your life may seem harsh for you as you read this book, but when you trust God and keep Him as the center of your love, you will not chase a fake. You can be strong and wait for the promise. Your promise from God is love. You can *Love Again*!

PRINCIPLE 2:

LET THE HEALING BEGIN

THE PROCESS OF HEALING CAN TAKE TIME, SO space must be allowed for the healing to take place. Many times, we carry pain behind a smile, struggling with the weight of an unjustifiable brokenness.

MANY TIMES, WE CARRY PAIN BEHIND A SMILE, STRUGGLING WITH THE WEIGHT OF AN UNJUSTIFIABLE BROKENNESS.

I have been witness to much hurt, pain, and brokenness. Some of the things that I witnessed, I wonder if I would have made it out myself. I admire the spiritual fortitude and inner strength of those who have endured love hurt and by God's help had to overcome. The images and stories of the broken yet remain in my mind. Imagine the young children who are left to mentally process the complexities of a marriage of Mom and Dad that didn't work, who watched the rapid deterioration of a relationship before their eyes between Mom and Dad that left a permanent scar on their souls. Imagine those children trying to reconcile where things went wrong and deeply questioning whether it's their own fault while they struggle to live through a dramatic life shift, somehow coming to grip with the fact that life and family will never be the same again. What they thought was true love is now in question. What they thought was real, they are now unsure about. There must be someone to blame for this hurt. There must be a source for the unwarranted piercing of the heart they carry deep within. Bitterness has now become their life poison of choice as they try to piece the puzzle of a life in a whirlwind back together. The truth is, it's not their fault, and it's not yours either. You can't blame yourself. You don't have all the answers. You can look for healing to come through the contrition of others, but what if that never happens? You can still be healed. In time, God has a way of bringing the right people into your life who will carry the word of healing in them. The word of healing they carry can be as simple as, "I'm sorry," from an individual who had nothing to do with the situation. It could be someone who chooses to love you while embracing all of your imperfections or a kind act that reaches the heart from a perfect stranger.

Healing may take time, but as your love for your Heavenly Father matures and grows those scars will heal, time will give way to the scab that is sure to fall off before you even realize it. One day when you check for it, you will be healed and whole.

Be Healed:

We do not have to die of a broken heart! Life can leave us scarred or wounded, and often, we use temporary fixes for hurts that require permanent healing. Growing up as a kid, I would somehow cut or scrape myself while playing outside. I recall running into the house to ask my mom or dad to look at my injury. Mom would use tender care and make sure that my cut or scrape was clean and cared for, and she would finish off by placing a bandage over the wound. Still wearing it days after the incident, Mom would say, "Take the bandage off so that the wound can finish healing properly!" Many of us have been wounded, have scars in our love lives, have spent many years wearing bandages, and yet have not experienced complete healing! Sometimes to be healed, we have to remove the bandage.

The bandages we use to cover wounds can be in the form of denial, unwillingness to trust, or insecurity that keeps us from loving ourselves. God wants to bring us to a place where the pain of our past will not prevent us from the brightness of our futures! Now is the time to remove all bandages and expose the wounds for the healing process.

GOD WANTS TO BRING US TO A PLACE WHERE THE PAIN OF OUR PAST WILL NOT PREVENT US FROM THE BRIGHTNESS OF OUR FUTURES!

The key to the proper healing of a wound is the environment in which one removes the bandage. It was important that my mom never undressed my wound while I was playing in the dirt because of the risk of further infection! In other words, we must be careful not to expose our wounds in atmospheres or among people who are not capable of healing us. At that very moment, we are in danger of hindering the healing process, exposing our hearts to more significant damage.

There is safety in the Master's arms and in His presence where the broken pieces of our lives begin to come together. Psalms 16:11 (KJV) states, "Thou [God] wilt shew me the path of life: in thy presence is fullness of joy; at thy right hand there are pleasures for evermore." Therefore, we should always uncover our wounds in the presence of God. He will not abuse us. He will not misuse us. He will not take advantage of us.

Take a moment to recall your love-life experiences (relationships, failures, rejections, etc.) that have created a negative impact on your view of true love. Be fully present and read the prayer that I prayed for you. "Father, I pray for my brother or sister reading this right now. I ask that Your presence fills the atmosphere around them. I ask You to use this time in Your presence to remove the bandages that have hidden their wounds and release total healing. In Jesus's name. Amen!" If you receive this prayer, I believe that God is moving upon you and within you to manifest the healing you need to *Love Again*!

PRINCIPLE 3:

LOVE IS
THE FUEL FOR
YOUR FAITH

THE MOST IMPORTANT RELATIONSHIP EVER TO be had is the vertical one between God and the believer. The connection between God and us is faith, "For without faith it is impossible to please Him" (Heb. 11:6 KJV). Has your faith ever been challenged? Do you feel there are roadblocks between you and a deeper relationship with Christ? These are moments we must examine *how* we love. An unfocused love life could mean an unfocused relationship with God. To bring clarity to our relationship with God, we have to let love be the fuel for our faith.

AN UNFOCUSED LOVE LIFE COULD MEAN AN
UNFOCUSED RELATIONSHIP WITH GOD.

Paul, in 1 Corinthians 13, declares the premium of what the love of God is. In verse 13, he makes clear the emphasis God places on love. When you read the full chapter, you will see how Paul pits love against several gifts and spiritual attributes. "Now abideth faith, hope, love, these three; but the greatest of these is love" (1 Cor. 13:13 NKJV). How can we say we love God whom we have not seen and hate our brother whom we see every day? When we love the way God wants us to love, then we can believe the way He wants us to believe.

There's something powerful about a pure, genuine love that flows from the heart. Song of Solomon 8:6 (KJV) says that "Love is strong as death." When God's love is flowing through us untainted by prejudice, pride, and paranoia, it will activate our faith to believe on a greater level that we could not have imagined. The purity of love is what lays at the core of our belief system. Our love causes us to believe even beyond the limits of death. That "God kind of love" is selfless, pushing you to believe, even when it's for someone else. Love ignites the fire of our faith.

LOVE IGNITES THE FIRE OF OUR FAITH.

The Tuesday Miracle:

My wife and I are blessed to enjoy two amazing, energetic, intelligent sons who always keep us on our toes. Every time I watch them participate in sports or play instruments, get into a little trouble (as most kids do) or excel in academics, I can't help but reflect on how good God has been to us through the years. The love you have for your children is special. It is a unique love that is sometimes hard to articulate. A true father and mother understand what it feels like when their children are hurting or in pain and they would rather take their place so they won't have to experience that excruciating hurt and anguish. In those moments, we find ourselves coming back to the sobering reality that you can't take the pain for them; you can't take their place. When my second son Tyler was just months old, he had a condition in his physical body that doctors could not figure out. Tyler's body would not gain the necessary weight for his age. He was eighteen months old and several months behind his projected growth. He was severely underweight, and it seemed to get worse and worse the more we tried. My wife and I went to doctor's visit after doctor's visit with no answers. We had gastro specialists and dietitians visit our home, but to no avail. Mom was doing everything in her power to help our son, but we were out of answers, out of patience, and mentally fatigued. We reached a point where all we could do was trust God. I can remember feeling helpless and lost, praying on how to move forward. No one could figure out what was going on, and it was frustrating. However, the one thing we had left was love. Love for our son, love for one another, love for God—love wouldn't let us stop believing, and searching for answers, trying to will our son to health.

It was a Tuesday night Bible study for us at church. We all got dressed and went to church while carrying the burden of our baby son who seemed to refuse to grow. For a moment, we felt like we didn't have any faith; we felt like doubt had written the ending of the story. Even in those desperate moments, love was still there. That night after Bible study, we shared what was happening with our pastor. Pastor asked my wife to bring our baby son Tyler down to a special place in the church we call the altar. Cradled in her arms and with tears in both of our eyes, we looked on, knowing that all we had left was love for our son. Love kept us believing that a miracle could happen for us. I remember that night, the seasoned mothers of the church began to gather around my son and my wife. One mother grabbed the blessed olive oil. Those seasoned mothers begin to rub my son with that oil and moans and hums of prayer started to be raised to the heavens. They began to pray circled around him as Pastor stood over his body from the pulpit and spoke a word of healing over his life and body. It was that night that we knew that we'd experienced a miracle. The pediatric appointment was about a week or so later. As my wife and I sat in the doctor's office, we saw her review the charts with a puzzled look. "I don't know what happened since the last visit," the doctor said. My wife and I immediately knew.

WHEN I THOUGHT MY FAITH HAD RUN DRY, THE
LOVE WAS STRONG IN ME, KINDLING THE FIRE
THAT BURNED IN THE CENTER OF OUR FAITH.

We knew our son Tyler had received a miracle. The condition was reversed; he was made whole. This is my experience. When I thought my faith had run dry, the love was strong in me, kindling the fire that burned in the center of our faith. Love will cause you to believe beyond limits in the face of adversity, even through the eye of the storm. Love became the fuel to our faith.

Love motivates our faith, our ministry, and what we do for God. We cannot afford to be a body of believers who are gifted but devoid of healthy love lives and relationships with God. When love motivates us, there is purity in our ministries, clarity in our words, and effectiveness in our discipleship. Love is the fuel for our faith; it is what makes our faith go! Galatians 5:6b speaks about how, "Faith works by love." When love fuels our belief, then we are most like our Father. When we consider the Father's relationship with us, His children, we see the example of His love for us. God had faith in us, our future, and what we could be through Him. God believed in us because He loved us. God's love for us prompted Him to act.

> *John 3:16 (KJV): "For God so loved the world that he gave his only begotten Son, that whosoever believeth in him should not perish, but have everlasting life."*

God gave His only. God gave His best. You see, that's what faith fueled by love is all about. When we are motivated and driven by the love of God in our hearts, it will cause us to act. When we are moved to action by love, then we are most like our Father.

PRINCIPLE 4:

HEART
PROBLEMS,
HEART FIXES

A SIGNIFICANT COMPONENT OF OUR ABILITY TO
love again and receive clarity in our "love lives" is to own and
confront the issues of our hearts. Let's keep it real—we all
have issues! The most dangerous issues are not physical
or within our bodies but are those issues that occur in our
hearts. Many times, we have difficulty dealing with heart-
level issues because of their emotional impact on our ability
to process them. In the introduction, I referenced Proverbs
4:23 from the Message Bible. The King James Version of
that scripture reads like this, "Keep thy heart with all diligence, for out of it are the issues of life."

PROTECTING AND SAFEGUARDING OUR HEARTS
IS A NATURAL RESPONSE TO POTENTIAL
THREATS OF HARM.

In context, the word *keep* means *to guard, to protect, and
to maintain* the heart. The word *diligence* denotes careful
and persistent work or effort. Protecting and safeguarding

our hearts is a natural response to potential threats of harm. However, in protecting our hearts, it behooves us to do so with the attentiveness it requires. Here is where diligence is most required—diligence to open ourselves to God to heal our hearts and diligence to maintain the healing and love of God *within* our hearts. Sometimes fixing a problem requires more time and effort than creating the problem itself! I often say, "Don't lose it in the moment." That is to say, many times, we make decisions in an instance that may have a long-term impact on us. As a result, we create a problem in a moment of passion that's going to take us much longer to work our way through.

Growing Pains:

It was after church. We had just had one of those hand-clapping, foot-stomping, tongue-talking "worship-fests" at my then-home church on Clay Street on the east side of Joliet, about twenty-five miles outside of Chicago. What happened then would serve as teachable moment for me. I believe that God always arranges teachable moments in life in order that we may grow and develop into the people He has called us to be. Allow me to give you a little backstory as to how I'd arrived at that powerhouse church on the east side of Joliet. I was only twelve years old when my father, who was already a full-time evangelist, had become the pastor of that small store-front church that would grow to become a banner and a beacon light of the community. I learned a lot at that place, and I have all the battle scars to prove it.

I WAS ONLY TWELVE YEARS OLD WHEN MY FATHER, WHO WAS ALREADY A FULL-TIME EVANGELIST, HAD BECOME THE PASTOR OF THAT SMALL STORE-FRONT CHURCH

I spent my early ministry years there under my father, Pastor Eugene Fears, Jr. You can always expect a powerful, life-altering experience to happen there every time you showed up. God knows Pastor Fears can preach you to a place of freedom, healing, and deliverance and out of whatever else is going on or wrong in your life. I had the amazing privilege of my natural father and my spiritual father being the same person, and I would often rely on him for guidance and wisdom (I still do). However, this Sunday, my greatest message that day would come after worship was over. You see, many times, our most poignant and impactful lessons in life happen when the music has ended, when the lights are off, and when the pews are empty. The reality is that when worship is over, you still must deal with "you." We must deal with our issues, our problems, and our personal short-comings and failures. Fellowship was an important part of what we did after every service—people talking, laughing, and having a good time. This particular Sunday was perfectly set up for me to learn more about myself. The lesson I had to learn centered on the truth that I had to get free from the often-unfair expectations of people and even sometimes the unfair expectations of myself. You see, I had to mature to love the man God created me to be. Well, sitting in the church after service, chatting, laughing, and discussing, I engaged in a very heated disagreement with someone close to me. Words were exchanged, and I was extremely upset and frustrated with the person because I felt that I had been mistreated and wronged. It didn't end well, to say the least. After days of boiling in the pot of my own feelings and emotions, I realized that I was having an unguarded moment. The problem I had was not with the loved-one who I thought had done me wrong; my problem was with me. It was the way I'd responded to the situation, how I'd let myself down, and how I'd left myself open to the criticism of not being who others wanted me to be.

<hr>

THE PROBLEM I HAD WAS NOT WITH THE LOVED-ONE WHO I THOUGHT HAD DONE ME WRONG; MY PROBLEM WAS WITH ME.

<hr>

It was the failure to live up to the unfair expectations of people. That was a heart problem for me. That unguarded moment helped me to learn that I had to allow God to be my measuring stick, that I control my response, and that the expectations of people cannot dictate my actions. I had a growth opportunity, a chance to learn how to mature in God's love. When God puts us in a position to heal and grow, He has to show us ourselves. We find ourselves standing in front of the mirror of God's perfect law of liberty, which is His Word, identifying and assessing how we need to grow to be who we were created to be. I discovered that we can hear and receive the opinions and thoughts of others about our lives without that opinion being the standard by which we are judged. The Word of God in our hearts is the standard and the bar. Psalms 119:11 (AMP) teaches us, "Your word I have treasured and stored in my heart, That I may not sin against You."

Sometimes, we make the mistake of thinking that all our problems are about everyone else when sometimes the problem is in us. This was a teachable moment for me, and I needed it.

While fixing problems is essential, there are other pressing matters of the heart to be fixed. Both Old and New Testament scriptures refer to the heart as the center of one's personality or spiritual life. The heart is known as the inner self that thinks, feels, and decides. Solomon pointed out in Proverbs 23:7, "For as he thinketh in his heart, so is he: Eat and drink, saith he to thee; but his heart is not with thee" (KJV). Furthermore, the heart carries our intentions. Take, for example, a young man courting a young lady. At some point in the pursuit, he will visit and meet the young lady's parents. Traditional parents are likely to ask, "Son, what are your intentions for our daughter?" This is a necessary question because the intentions of the heart are not easily revealed or uncovered.

Let's consider this a little further. Sometimes relationships can be misjudged because of the intentions of our hearts. How many times have we entered a relationship with the wrong plans, therefore misinterpreting the proper purpose of the connection? It can be a tricky thing because intentions are not always easily discerned nor expressed. As a result, two people can be in the same relationship and have different purposes. Perhaps this is why individuals in relationships guard their hearts, to avoid hurt.

GOD LOVES US SO MUCH THAT HE PUTS US IN A POSITION TO RELY UPON THE PROMISE THAT HIS WORD WILL DISCERN FOR US THE PROPER INTENTIONS OF OUR HEART AND RELATIONSHIPS.

I'll reiterate here why our relationship with God must be a priority. Inclusive of our relationship with Him is an interconnectedness with His Word. Studying Scripture helps us see what is in our hearts and allows us to avoid our most damaging decisions. When we have ill or misguided intentions in our hearts, we will act on them unless God reveals what is right and what is wrong. God loves us so much that He puts us in a position to rely upon the promise that His Word will discern for us the proper intentions of our heart and relationships. As a result of this discernment, we can make targeted, life-giving decisions. Hebrews 4:12 greatly encourages me regarding the power of God's Word. "For the word of God is quick, and powerful, and sharper than any two-edged sword, piercing even to the dividing asunder of soul and spirit, and of the joints and marrow, and is a discerner of the thoughts and intents of the heart."

I am sure that we have all lived through various experiences where misguided intentions and other issues have taken an emotional toll on us. Many lessons are learned from such moments. We can look back on learned lessons and see how God kept us from ourselves and the consequences of poor decisions. His keeping us is a reason to be grateful because He allowed us to come through that wrong love decision without it destroying us but instead, used it to make us strong enough to embrace His purpose for our lives.

We should ask God for a pure heart to love the way He wants us to because without it, we can miss Him. Matthew 5:8 (KVJ) declares, "Blessed are the pure in heart: for they shall see God." Not only see Him in eternal life to come but see Him in our present lives and relationships. It does take a pure heart. Therefore, we must allow the Word of God to cleanse us so we can make the best choices. The prophet Jeremiah stated, "The heart is deceitful above all things, and desperately wicked: who can know it?" (Jer. 17:9 KJV). You must trust the heart of God within you, allowing your life to be governed in principle by His Word.

PRINCIPLE 5:

RECOVERY
FROM HEART
MISTAKES

HEART MISTAKES HAPPEN. WE ALL HAVE TO experience them. Sometimes, we simply make the wrong choice with our hearts because we leave our hearts unguarded. A great example of this is King David's recovery from a heart mistake in 2 Samuel 11. While walking on his rooftop, David noticed the beautiful Bathsheba taking a bath in her home. At that moment, the contents of David's heart were challenged. His yielding to the carnal desires within resulted in one of his biggest mistakes. As the king, he requested Bathsheba be brought to him. The problem— she was the wife of another man, Uriah, who was a valiant soldier in David's army.

Recall from Hebrews 4:12 that the Word is the discerner of the intentions of the heart. Here's a case in point as David dealt with a heart mistake. In chapter 12 of 2 Samuel, David received a word through Nathan the prophet whom God used to let David know that He was aware of his folly and poor decisions regarding Bathsheba and Uriah. David went on to suffer the loss of the son he and Bathsheba shared, likely as a consequence of his mistake. However, in such a dark moment, David left us an example of how to recover from a heart mistake.

Ultimately, David revealed the sincere desire of his heart, right standing with God. He threw himself at the mercy of God, which we all must do when we find ourselves in need of His help. You will be blessed by reading David's recovery process in Psalm 51. His prayer became that God would wash him of his iniquity. We, like David, should be courageous enough to ask God to reveal to and cleanse us of the hidden things in our hearts. This requires the willingness to acknowledge our transgressions and the humility to ask for forgiveness and be cleansed of our sins. We must look at ourselves in the mirror and admit what we have done. David confessed, (Ps. 51:4a KJV) "Against thee, thee only, have I sinned." We have to acknowledge and own our sins and errors!

WE, LIKE DAVID, SHOULD BE COURAGEOUS ENOUGH TO ASK GOD TO REVEAL TO AND CLEANSE US OF THE HIDDEN THINGS IN OUR HEARTS.

You can be as David right now and recover from any heart mistake. With God, you are free to uncover frailty and fault, knowing that in your weakness, God makes you strong. I don't know about you, but I do not want to spend time going in the wrong direction when God is trying to move me forward. You can turn this thing around! It's not too bad, you are not too far gone, it's not over, and you can recover from this!

Simply stated, we have to be real with God! His desire for us is that we would have truth in our hearts, or as David put it, God desires truth in the inward part. The inward part is the place others cannot see. So, with all your heart and with everything you have, cry out to God and ask Him to, "Create in me a clean heart, oh God, and renew in me a right spirit" (Ps. 51:10 KJV). That's the best way to begin to love again. His very response helps us realize just how much we need Him!

As we learn from the story and interaction of King David, a heart mistake can be damaging, if not fatal. It's not a stretch to say that sometimes your heart cannot be trusted. How many times have we found ourselves in situations where we have made permanent decisions with our hearts and not our heads? It is possible to ignore signs and signals of a potential heart mistake that may be glaringly obvious to others on the outside and yet hidden to those involved. Let's revisit Jeremiah chapter 17 and take a deeper look:

> *Jeremiah 17:9-10 (NLT): "[9] The human heart is the most deceitful of all things, and desperately wicked. Who really knows how bad it is? [10] But I, the LORD, search all hearts and examine secret motives. I give all people their due rewards, according to what their actions deserve."*

The Word of God teaches us the lesson that the heart is deceitful and cannot always be relied on. The Lord knows and understands the hearts of men, drilling down to the core of our secret motives. The motives of the heart are evidenced by our actions. Our minds can tell us one thing, and our hearts will say another. This is precisely how heart mistakes can occur. One of the keys to recovery is understanding how we got there in the first place. What are our true motives emanating from the heart? Asking ourselves the tough questions is how we begin recovery.

What David experienced in the Scriptures is not all that uncommon; it happens every day. You may be in a position today where you are broken and in need of recovery from a heart mistake.

James' Story:

I had an incredible opportunity to have a conversation with a dear friend, who we will refer to as James. James opened up a slice of his life to me as I pursued the passionate journey of gathering testimony, relevant research, my own personal experiences, as well as the relationship experiences of others to powerfully convey the message of *Love Again*. The experiences and research I gathered were from those who were able to learn, heal, and overcome heart mistakes.

Let's look at James' personal story. I only observed my friend James from a distance as it relates to some of the things he experienced and endured in his most private and intimate relationships. It was not always my place to be directly involved in what was very personal to him. As

James opened up to me about his life, what I learned from his unique perspective about heart mistakes in relationships further reminded me that many of us have dealt and wrestled with some of the same heart mistakes that now serve as our shared life experiences.

The Scriptures remind us in 1 Corinthians 10:13 (NLT), "The temptations in your life are no different from what others experience. And God is faithful. He will not allow the temptation to be more than you can stand. When you are tempted, he will show you a way out so that you can endure." In other words, we all will face tests and trials that we must learn to overcome and grow from.

The conversation I had with James provided powerful insight into relationship situations many of us have experienced. Let's examine a very candid conversation James and I had as we began to discuss various aspects of the impact of our relationships with God and with others. As I was writing and meditating about recovery from heart mistakes, I wanted to dive a little deeper into James' real-life situations and experiences. The following is a brief highlight of some of the impactful and resonating moments and key takeaways of the story of James' personal heart mistakes and ultimate recovery.

James shared with me that he experienced some very low and dark moments as a result of heart mistakes. In his pursuit of love, his actions and behaviors became a toxic cycle of troubled relationships. *How did it happen? How did I get here?* Those were some of the poignant questions that seemed to run through James' mind as he reflected on those life-testing moments.

IN HIS PURSUIT OF LOVE, HIS ACTIONS
AND BEHAVIORS BECAME A TOXIC CYCLE
OF TROUBLED RELATIONSHIPS. *HOW DID IT
HAPPEN? HOW DID I GET HERE?*

"Sometimes I realize that my heart mistakes didn't only come from an emotional place of my heart but rather began in the thought arena of the heart," James said. This is a fundamental truth that the Word of God supports; how we think in our inner place is who we are.

> *Proverbs 23:7a: "For as He thinks in His heart, so is he."*

James went on to recount his relationship experiences that drove him to a place in his mind and life that he never wanted to be. When we make heart mistakes, most times it is not our intent to do so when we entered into the relationship in the first place. James discovered as he was in the throes of unstable relationships that he had overanalyzed what to do and what not to do. James was trying to find his way in relationships that eventually caused him to be led by carnal desires. He made decisions that triggered him to be trapped in the web of mixed motives and imprecise thinking. Those thoughts became actions which caused James to put himself in a compromised position in his life and relationship with God and others.

The mixed emotions and wrong thoughts that James had in his heart made him think that the problem was with others when in fact, the problem was within him. He was trying to change others when he needed God to change him. When we think that we can change a person on our own and without the power of God's love involved, it can result in the leading of oneself into a black hole of inconsistency and destructive decisions. His initial thoughts that at first seemed harmless led to constant actions that were uncontrollable. He found himself engaging in a level of intimacy that ultimately created ungodly soul ties and more misleading emotions that had him spiraling out of mental and emotional control. This cycle of behavior would lead to his relationships falling apart. James would lose his way. *"It was breaking me down physically, and it killed me spiritually."* The destructive behaviors started with one thought that became action and led to the deterioration of James' mental capacity, spiritual well-being, emotional well-being, and physical health.

The Road to Recovery:

What I learned from James' story is that trying to make the right decision on what to do next is very difficult when you're in that dark place; it causes stress on the body and even many thoughts that don't even seem like your own. You may be reading this book today and you're in that dark place—that vicious cycle of anguish that a heart mistake can leave you in, sitting in the stew of your own disgust and frustration.

Before you know it, just as James did, you will find yourself wondering how you got here. It's very easy to get into a tough place of emotional hurt and heart mistakes, but it is even harder to get out. As I talked with James, we both acknowledged and understood through our conversation that there was a realization early in those relationships that he was headed down the wrong road; however, he couldn't get himself out. The relationships he was in were prompted by wrong motives and consequently turned into a life of frustration and sleepless nights. James, as many of us do, spent significant time and energy camouflaging in front of everyone what was going on to convince himself that he was okay.

In James' own words, he stated: "*I was trying to make it as though I was playing a trick on my heart. I was trying to rest, but was in a place I knew I wasn't supposed to be. I was emotionally bound; I didn't want to hurt the other person. I was in a dark place, and while you're in there, you don't realize how dark it is. The problem is that when your heart feels like you're making a good decision, you begin to mask abuse, both verbal, and physical. You find yourself going to other sources, trying to fill the void that started with one bad decision of the heart.*"

You can imagine how difficult it was for James to recount this hurtful experience and season of his life. We can all learn from this transparent and introspective look and can take this moment to examine our hearts and see how we came to the place of a heart mistake in order to start the road to recovery.

Some way and somehow, you have to battle your way out of that bad space caused by a heart mistake. You must fight, even claw your way out and make the sacrifice for your freedom. Dr. Martin Luther King Jr. once said, *"If you can't fly then run, if you can't run then walk, if you can't walk then crawl, but whatever you do you have to keep moving forward."* (King, Martin. 1960. "Keep Moving from This Mountain." *Address at Spelman College* (April).

James' road to recovery from a heart mistake is a path that many of us must take. Ultimately, recovery is a process. James victoriously spoke of his recovery from his personally experienced heart mistake and how he has now gained victory in his life. The process starts with changing your thoughts and then taking the steps, however small they be, toward your freedom and victory. In the natural sense, heart disease is typically a result of bad habits and decisions left untreated over a lengthy period of time. In many life situations, this is also true of recovery from a heart mistake. There must be a process of making good decisions consistently over time that align with God's Word and will for your life. We must use God's Word as the authority that will keep our thoughts under subjection, arresting every destructive and negative thought.

> *2 Corinthians 10:5 (NLT): "We destroy every proud obstacle that keeps people from knowing God. We capture their rebellious thoughts and teach them to obey Christ."*

The pursuit of love and trying to find "the one" can be a slippery slope. You find yourself trying to manage your emotions and make clear decisions, all while trying to learn and cultivate a relationship with another person.

WE MUST USE GOD'S WORD AS THE AUTHORITY THAT WILL KEEP OUR THOUGHTS UNDER SUBJECTION, ARRESTING EVERY DESTRUCTIVE AND NEGATIVE THOUGHT.

We have all been there, and that is why we must be settled in ourselves and anchored in our relationship with God so that we won't travel the wrong road. James' heart mistake left him traveling that wrong road in pursuit of love, trying to find the one. In taking a deeper look into James' heart mistake, I discovered a jarring experience that was at the core of his actions and behavior.

When James was five years old, his parents entrusted a local church family to babysit him. James was molested by the man of the house, who was also a preacher. This experience resulted in confusion for young James. He understood the dysfunction of what had taken place but hid it for many years. That horrific experience birthed the seed of resentment, unbalanced emotions, and James' inability to control and express the way he loved in relationships. Consequently, this opened James' heart to the lifelong personal demons that he had to battle. It was difficult for James to escape from this. One of the manifestations, in James' words, of this negative encounter was the spirit of lust that dominated what he saw, his thoughts, and his desires. The seed that had been planted those years ago did not allow him to love from a place of purity because the negative attachment overrode his ability to love people with a sincere and true heart. It manifested itself in lies, deceitfulness, and unfaithfulness because he was controlled by the negative spirit of his past. It wasn't until he lost out on a lot of friendships and great relationships and realized how many people he had hurt because he was hurt that he knew he needed change. He needed to be put on the right track to love and heal. Recovery was necessary.

IN THE PROCESS OF RECOVERY, PRAYER BECOMES PARAMOUNT BECAUSE ULTIMATELY, WE MUST EMPTY OUR HEARTS OUT TO GOD.

In the process of recovery, prayer becomes paramount because ultimately, we must empty our hearts out to God. Prayer is not a monologue but rather a dialogue with God where we both hear and receive instruction from our Father and Creator. We must ask God to take out of us what doesn't belong, surrendering ourselves in complete humility to the One who can heal us and change us. We must be 100 percent honest with God and true to ourselves. Without this type of candid transparency and authenticity a heart mistake can cause depression, brokenness, and other weights that keep us shackled and bound. In James' case, he was still actively involved in his local church, still singing and still serving, yet bound in spirit because of a heart mistake.

Difficult decisions must be made that sometimes require you to remove yourself from a comfortable and familiar situation, totally freeing yourself of distractions that will keep you from full recovery. When you make these real, practical, tangible steps, *now it's time to heal; now it's time to grow.*

The road to recovery starts with one decision. You understand you can't do it on your own. You must surround yourself with people that can help, support, and tell you the truth.

James' childhood hurt, failures, and disappointments that he'd never addressed and confronted left him struggling in present relationships. James realized that he had seen many bad relationship decisions made throughout his life and found himself making the same mistakes he'd witnessed. To heal and recover, you must be willing to seek wise counsel and help, even in uncomfortable situations, in order to find healing. Dealing with a change of environment and challenging your norm may be a culture shock, but if you stick with it, you will be able to heal.

I asked James, "How are you maintaining?"

James responded:

> *"By staying focused. You still have to watch.*
> *You know what the situation looks like based*
> *on your past experience. If you're not alert*
> *and aware, you are at risk to be broken again.*
> *You have to prayerfully change your behavior,*
> *finding your direction in the Word of God."*

Through James' personal experience, we learn that your desire to change and taking the steps for recovery will be the catalyst of freedom and healing for you. Go forward and live your change.

PRINCIPLE 6:

LOVING
YOURSELF

WHEN WE LEARN TO LOVE GOD PROPERLY, HE teaches us to respect ourselves deeply. However, many of us never walk in this self-respect, which causes us to abuse relationships with others. Remember, the Bible teaches us to love our neighbors as we love ourselves. If we devalue ourselves, harm our own lives, and lack self-worth, we are bound to reciprocate that to others.

WE SOMETIMES SETTLE FOR ANYTHING AND
TAKE UNNECESSARY ABUSE BECAUSE WE DON'T
LOVE OURSELVES!

We can only respect people to the extent that we respect ourselves. The countless number of men and women who end up in a place of vulnerability due to the lack of value they place upon themselves is unfortunate. We sometimes settle for anything and take unnecessary abuse because we don't love ourselves! We are fearfully and wonderfully made, created in the image and likeness of God. We do have something unique to offer! We cannot afford to have a distorted view of our own lives. God created such greatness in us, and we must see it in ourselves.

We tend to attract who we are or whom we project to be. Sometimes we draw insecure people because we are uncertain of ourselves. We invite the fearful when we are afraid. However, today is where it ends! Declare with me, "I am going to see myself how God sees me!" When you begin viewing yourself from God's point of view, not only will your choices change, but the way you respond to the perceptions of who you are will change! The people you attract will also change because you will reflect the purity of love you have for yourself and the Father. Remember, God loves you. He is concerned about you, and you do not have to be less than what He has called and created you to be.

Make This Declaration:

Make this declaration today and in the days to come, "I am going to be whom God has called me to be. I am going to love myself. I am not going to abuse myself. I am beautiful in God. I have a good heart. I have a healed heart. My passion is for God. I have something special to offer." If you allow Jesus to teach you how to love, you will never love wrong again.

MAKE THIS DECLARATION TODAY AND IN THE DAYS TO COME, "I AM GOING TO BE WHOM GOD HAS CALLED ME TO BE. I AM GOING TO LOVE MYSELF. I AM NOT GOING TO ABUSE MYSELF. I AM BEAUTIFUL IN GOD. I HAVE A GOOD HEART. I HAVE A HEALED HEART. MY PASSION IS FOR GOD. I HAVE SOMETHING SPECIAL TO OFFER." IF YOU ALLOW JESUS TO TEACH YOU HOW TO LOVE, YOU WILL NEVER LOVE WRONG AGAIN.

Rejection:

We hardly ever talk about it, it's not easy to articulate, and many times, we are reluctant to admit it. Rejection! If you had a golden shovel of the heart that could dig through the callused layers of pain and emotional wounds and scars, you would probably find resting at the foundation of this complex center of the human soul the residue of rejection. Here is where it gets a little tough, but hold on, and I promise this will help. Rejection is what we internalize and tuck away, hoping to never bring to the forefront the thought of how it made us feel. Rejection is a dangerous cancer because if left unaddressed, it will spread, infecting everything in its path. Rejection is about acceptance. *Am I accepted like I am? Do I fit in? Will they like me? Am I good enough?* All of us have dealt with some form of rejection that has led to us licking our wounds time and time again. Rejection can come from a parent or not being allowed in the "in" crowd or even a system or organization.

IF WE INTEND TO EXPERIENCE HEALING
OF THE HEART, WE MUST BIND THE
STRONGMAN OF REJECTION.

The reality is that many of us have just learned to cope with the killer sting of rejection. The scary part is that rejection resting at the core of your heart often leads to behaviors that truly do not represent who God has made you to be. As it relates to matters of the heart, rejection is a strong man.

> *Mark 3:27 (MEV): "No one can enter a strong man's house and plunder his goods, unless he first binds the strong man. Then he will plunder his house."*

If we intend to experience healing of the heart, we must bind the strongman of rejection. Oftentimes, rejection can lead to low-self-esteem and low self-worth. It can also lead to an unhealthy view of our own valuable attributes.

I, like so many others, spent my teen years trying to discover who I was. I remember it well. Some of you have stories similar to my own. As a pastor's kid, I had a full-time night life—Bible class, revival, state meeting, conventions—yes, a night life! I really enjoyed it. However, I had to figure out how to adjust to my day life. As a young person growing up, you spend most of your teen years trying to fit in somewhere. What crowd did I belong to at school? What life did I want to live on my neighborhood block? How could I live up to expectations of a PK (preacher's kid)? Rejection became the fierce battle that I had to navigate through during those times. I was able to function and enjoy my life; however, you always remember the pain of trying to be accepted.

During my senior year of high school, I was walking across the auditorium stage to receive a quarterly award. I had on my wide leg jeans (in style at the time), my blue sweater vest with a blue checked shirt, and, to top it off, a clear frame, yellow-tent, non-prescription pair of glasses. I was really feeling my style! I was walking confidently, checking out the world, being myself. Why is this even important? It's important because that was the moment I began the journey of understanding who I was. I was figuring out what I liked. In that moment walking across the stage, I was beginning to be okay with myself and starting to embrace the person God had made me to be, and once

ONCE YOU UNDERSTAND AND REALIZE THAT YOUR FATHER HAS ALREADY ACCEPTED YOU, THEN YOU ARE FREE FROM THE POWER OF THOSE WHO DO NOT.

I began to embrace that person, rejection began to break. You see, the strength of rejection lies in a longing for acceptance. Once you understand and realize that your Father has already accepted you, then you are free from the power of those who do not. The power of the Father's acceptance, if you allow it, can be a healing balm to your heart, eradicating the grip and stronghold of rejection.

> *Ephesians 1:5-6 KJV: "Having predestinated*
> *us unto the adoption of children by Jesus*
> *Christ to himself, according to the good plea-*
> *sure of his will, To the praise of the glory of*
> *his grace, wherein he hath made us accepted*
> *in the beloved."*

Predestination means what was determined before, adoption speaks to an intentional choice, and good pleasure means that your Father God was happy to do it. Simply put, you have already been accepted by God.

THE TRUTH OF GOD'S PREDETERMINATION OF
OUR LIVES, HIS CHOICE OF US, AND HIS GOOD
PLEASURE TO ACCEPT US IS LIBERATING.

This truth opens the light of freedom to our dark souls and destroys rejection. The truth of God's predetermination of our lives, His choice of us, and His good pleasure to accept us is liberating. Your Heavenly Father accepted you, regardless of what you look like and what you've done. You are accepted, in spite of your past and your family background. You are accepted, even though you may be awkward and find it difficult to fit in. No matter what, you are accepted. Just like I did in high school during that awards ceremony, take a walk across your life stage; embrace who you were created to be. Express your uniqueness and confidently walk in full view of the world, knowing rejection has no place in your heart because you were already accepted by God before it even had a chance!

PRINCIPLE 7:

GO FORWARD

ONE OF THE INCREDIBLE THINGS ABOUT MAR-riage is the fact that you get to have shared experiences. It is the merging of two backgrounds, two histories, and two ways of doing things. Each person must collaborate to make one artistic masterpiece called marriage. One of the remarkable things I have been able to witness through my marriage has been the trial, struggle, and victory my wife has experienced. She has been a glaring example to me of how to love again.

At the age of only six years old, my wife experienced a life-altering situation in her family. Her father was addicted to drugs, and her mother had to move her family away to a safe place for their survival. Consequently, for twenty-three years or more after, her father chose not to be a part of their lives. My wife and I were well into our marriage with two children when she was reunited with her father. I finally had the opportunity to meet my father-in-law, and our sons, their grandfather. My wife made a remarkable statement just before this experience. She said, "No matter how I feel about what he did or how I feel about what we had to go through, I decided to forgive and love him anyway!" Talk about loving again and moving forward—*wow!* At that moment, my wife helped me learn a valuable, powerful, life-changing lesson. From that point on, after all those years, my wife and her father began to build a relationship fit for them. This was exemplified as she loved her father through the end of his life.

> "NO MATTER HOW I FEEL ABOUT WHAT HE DID OR HOW I FEEL ABOUT WHAT WE HAD TO GO THROUGH, I DECIDED TO FORGIVE AND LOVE HIM ANYWAY!"

Many of us deal with unexplainable hurt and pain primarily because of situations we cannot control. We merely learn how to carry it with heavy hearts and battled minds, but forgiveness is the key. When we forgive, there is a supernatural release that frees our minds and sets our spirits free. Forgiveness is the green light to move forward in life and is the turning point to love again. Now that the healing process is in full motion, it's time to *Love Again!*

We must be careful to ensure that we don't make the same mistakes but learn from our life's experiences. How many times have we missed the lesson and had to retake the test?

FORGIVENESS IS THE GREEN LIGHT TO MOVE FORWARD IN LIFE AND IS THE TURNING POINT TO LOVE AGAIN.

Graduation Time:

I believe you are reading *7 Principles to Love Again* because you are ready to graduate to the next level in life. You have made enough mistakes, you've had enough hard knocks, you've compromised enough, and you now realize it is time for you to be whole! Psalm 147:3 says, "He (God) healeth the broken in heart, and bindeth up their wounds" (KJV). I believe there is a special power from God that can fix your heart. The Spirit of God has a way of touching you in the deepest part of your heart that only He can reach. I don't know about you, but in my life, there are some things that only God can handle. Amen?

Scripture reminds me of the power that comes through Jesus Christ to heal the heart. Isaiah 61:1 says, "The Spirit of the Lord GOD is upon me; because the LORD hath anointed me to preach good tidings unto the meek; he hath sent me to bind up the brokenhearted, to proclaim liberty to the captives, and the opening of the prison to them that are bound." The Spirit of the Lord is here and will heal your heart so that you can love again!

WHEN YOU CAN RECALL WHERE YOU FELL, YOU CAN BE POISED NOT TO BE IN THAT PLACE AGAIN.

Beloved, let's make sure that we put this into practice. We cannot only agree mentally with these words, but we must also apply these powerful, God-given precepts to our daily living. In Revelation 2:1-5, John recorded the words of Christ as He spoke to the church in Ephesus. You will note all the great things and commendable actions of the church of Ephesus. However, in all of its commendable actions, Jesus said that He had something against them as they had left their first love—God Himself! The instructions for their redemption were simple: recall where you fell, repent, and do your early works again. Applying this cure is essential for us to move forward. Can you remember the point that you lost it? Can you remember the relationship that took everything out of you? Can you recall the decision that put you in your most vulnerable place? When you can recall where you fell, you can be poised not to be in that place again.

THE PRAYER TO CHANGE DIRECTION:
REPENTANCE IS JUST AS SIMPLE AS YOU TALKING
TO GOD FROM YOUR HEART AND SAYING, "LORD,
I ACKNOWLEDGE MY WRONG. I AM CHANGING
MY WAYS, AND WITH YOUR HELP, I CAN FOLLOW
YOUR LEAD." IF YOU PRAY THIS PRAYER RIGHT
NOW, THERE IS ENOUGH GRACE AND MERCY FOR
YOU TO GO FORWARD. DO YOUR FIRST WORKS
AGAIN AND RENEW YOUR COMMITMENT TO
BEING DEVOTED TO A SINCERE RELATIONSHIP
WITH GOD. SIMPLY STATED, PUT GOD FIRST!

If going forward I can keep myself in the right places and around the right people, I will avoid situations that would lead me back to hurt and brokenness. Repent means to turn and to change direction. It is the acknowledgment that the actions we took were wrong in God's sight. Moreover, it shows our reliance on the help of God.

The Prayer to Change Direction:

Repentance is just as simple as you talking to God from your heart and saying, "Lord, I acknowledge my wrong. I am changing my ways, and with Your help, I can follow Your lead." If you pray this prayer right now, there is enough grace and mercy for you to go forward. Do your first works again and renew your commitment to being devoted to a sincere relationship with God. Simply stated, put God first!

I will conclude with an illustration from a story found in St. John Chapter 8, a woman caught in the act of adultery. According to the Law of Moses, this was an offense punishable by stoning. She was in a place of embarrassment at the feet of Jesus. Sometimes, it is difficult to deal with your issues when shame is staring you in the face. Yet, Jesus dealt with the woman from a place of love and forgiveness. He wrote in the ground and reminded the accusers of their human frailties and dealt with her accusers and her condemnation. Jesus later looked up and asked the woman, "Where are those accusers and has no man condemned you?" The woman responded, 'No man Lord.' And Jesus said, 'Neither do I condemn thee! Go and sin no more.'" (St. John 8:10-11 KJV)

As you begin to walk into this new place in your life, loving the way God wants you to, don't worry about your critics and naysayers. Jesus will deal with all of your accusers. There is no need to walk in condemnation once you begin to do things God's way. I want you to know that your instructions and commandments from heaven are to go forward!

THERE IS NO NEED TO WALK IN CONDEMNATION
ONCE YOU BEGIN TO DO THINGS GOD'S WAY.

Your past is over, you are healed in your present, and your future is bright. As much time as it may take, do your part and let Jesus do the rest; then you can *Love Again*! God is love, and as long as He is in your life, it is never over!